"Among the most important biblical truths for children to understand as they grow are those surrounding what God has done, and is doing now, to bring sinners to a secure place of faith in Christ. *PROOF Pirates* provides an engaging and creative format for presenting these truths and invites parents and children alike to live the story of God's grace. Parents will be grateful for the clear and faithful presentation of these truths, based on biblical teaching, and children will revel in the story format that welcomes their active participation. Families will be strengthened and encouraged as they enter into the world of this enjoyable, creative, and biblically faithful devotional."

BRUCE A. WARE, Professor of Christian Theology, Southern Seminary, and Author of *Big Truths for Young Hearts*

"Family devotional time can be overwhelming. Sharing God's big truths with little hearts is not an easy task. *PROOF Pirates Family Devotional* has changed the game by making devotional time fun and full of gospel goodness. Your heart will be encouraged as you share the Good News with your children."

JESSICA THOMPSON, Speaker; coauthor of *Give Them Grace*

"*PROOF Pirates* is an exciting way for kids to discover the truth of God's Grace. Best of all, this is a treasure hunt they can share as a family. This playful story and excellent illustrations will bring home the meaning of the gospel in a way children won't soon forget. What family can resist secret clues, a pirate adventure, and solid Bible teaching?"

TONY KUMMER, Editor at Ministry-To-Children, Missions Pastor at Calvary Baptist of Madison, IN; father of eight aspiring pirates

"Parenting shortcomings teach us to drink deeply of God's grace or else drown in shame of not living up or 'getting it right.' *PROOF Pirates* is beautifully illustrated and memorably worded to be both fun and instructional for the whole family. As God teaches us about his grace in parenting, let us teach and parent our children with grace and pirates!"

DANIEL MONTGOMERY, Lead Pastor of Sojourn Community Church in Louisville, KY; founder of the Sojourn Network; author of *Faithmapping* and *PROOF*

"*PROOF Pirates* is a ch[...] on their shelf. The wo[...] ture your children's imagination as the deep truth, simply presented, introduces them to God's amazing grace. The well-written, activity-packed family devotions that follow the story are what make *PROOF Pirates a* family treasure your kids are sure to love and will read again and again."

MARTY MACHOWSKI, Family Life Pastor; author of the *Gospel Story for Kids* series and *The Ology: Ancient Truths Ever New*

"What an important truth for kids to hear: that their worth comes from Jesus, not their performance! And what a fun way to tell it! This is the rare family resource that puts rich teaching about God's grace in a playful, engaging book. Who would have thought good theology could be this much fun?"

JACK KLUMPENHOWER, Author of *Show Them Jesus*; coauthor of *What's Up?* and *The Gospel-Centered Parent*

"Imagine a new generation of evangelicals who, from their childhood, have known the sacred writings and sound theology, and have experienced the overwhelming grace of God in their daily lives. They're not concerned about religious performance, they aren't moralists, they don't believe that their good behavior can earn God's favor, and they don't suffer from legalism. *PROOF Pirates* will go a long way to raising up that next generation!"

GREGG R. ALLISON, Professor of Christian Theology, The Southern Baptist Theological Seminary; pastor, Sojourn Community Church, Louisville, KY; Secretary, the Evangelical Theological Society; author

"Kids need PROOF of God's amazing grace, and this fun little book will remind them of exactly that. Get a copy for your kids today!"

DEEPAK REJU, Pastor of Counseling and Family Ministry, Capitol Hill Baptist Church; author of *Great Kings of the Bible* and *On Guard*

"*PROOF Pirates* is a fun way to learn profound truths about God's grace and salvation. My kids loved it! One was even bouncing up and down in anticipation of the next clue. Resources like this which are so engaging and biblically faithful are great gifts for families, and I am grateful for people who produce them."

RAY VAN NESTE, Professor of Biblical Studies, Union University

"This creative and well-illustrated children's book winsomely presents the 'doctrines of grace' to the next generation. It includes kid-friendly family devotionals to accompany each doctrinal point covered. Highly recommended."

ROBERT L. PLUMMER, Professor of New Testament Interpretation, The Southern Baptist Theological Seminary

"*PROOF Pirates* is a book that explains the depths of God's grace in ways children (and even parents) can easily understand. This is the kind of treasure I've been waiting for and parents have been looking for! The story is easy for children to get into and the devotional is easy for parents to use. The VBS will be equally incredible, I'm sure!"

PAT ALDRIDGE, Community Life Pastor, Redeemer Fellowship, St. Charles, IL. Blogger at pataldridge.com and gospelcenteredfamily.com

"As a father of three, I'm always on the investigative trail for those tools that can help clarify the message of grace to my family. The *PROOF Pirates Family Devotional* is one of those very items! The clear and playful explanation of what the gospel means to all of us is perfectly laid out in a way to start these very important forever conversations."

JONATHAN CLIFF, Pastor of Community, Grace Community Church, Clarksville, TN

"The *PROOF Pirates* devotional is a delightful, grace-filled adventure that will help remind young (and old) spiritual scallywags that there is an amazing God in heaven who loves them and wants to lavish undeserved favor on them through Christ. It does a wonderful job of explaining the vast, deep doctrine of grace at a child's level and forcing

works-based righteousness to walk the plank. The devotional is insightful, fun and practical, offering lots of great, pirate-themed activities to illustrate key truths. I encourage you to set sail on the high seas of God's grace with this latest treasure from the children's ministry team at Sojourn!"

JOSHUA COOLEY, Children's Minister; author of *One Year Devotions with Jesus* and *Heroes of the Bible Devotional*

"I plan to put a copy of *PROOF Pirates* in the hands of every parent in our church because I'm convinced there's no more important thing that parents can help their children discover than God's amazing grace. It's my prayer that God will use this engaging devotional to remind parents of the astonishing reality of this grace and to awaken little hearts to the wonder and beauty of our gracious God."

MIKE CROWE, Associate Minister of Families, Shades Mountain Independent Church, Birmingham, AL

"My family enjoyed going through this great family devotional! *PROOF Pirates* engages kids' imaginations while teaching them about God's multifaceted grace. This book is an excellent resource for any parent desiring to help their family memorize Scripture, pray, and learn about God's character. Go on a treasure hunt and discover the PROOF of God's grace!"

JEFF HUTCHINGS, Pastor of Family Ministry, The Journey—Tower Grove

"There are few things kids and parents both need to understand like grace. True grace. Costly grace. The authors have produced a tool that distills the message of God's lavish grace in a way that parents can practically share with their kids through activities and accessible language. I am grateful for their work and the benefit it will be to the church in general and my family in particular."

SAM LUCE, Family Pastor, Redeemer Church, Utica, NY

"It's not often that an introduction to a children's book grabs me but this one did. And all because of the line 'Jesus came to save sinners—not those who get everything right.' This message saturates *PROOF Pirates* and reading it has backed up a lifetime's lesson that the gospel is the greatest treasure there is. We need to rediscover lessons like this even as adults, and especially if we wish to teach the next generation about the love of God. I can so easily picture boys and girls reading *PROOF Pirates* and growing up with this truth—that God saves sinners. I can see families learning together the foundational truth of God's plan for salvation. *PROOF Pirates* reminded me of this wonderful God given-gift, and it is something I can't wait to read aloud to my nieces and nephews."

CATHERINE MACKENZIE, Author and editor, Christian Focus 4 Kids

"*PROOF Pirates* is a creative and useful family devotional for parents looking to help their kids understand and internalize the truth about God's love! Jesse's journey is filled with clever adventures that reveal God's grace to him in tactile, fun ways. Kids—and their parents!—will enjoy following along with Jesse and learning more about God!"

MELANIE B. RAINER, Director of Content, Creative Trust; editor, *What's in the Bible?* curriculum; and coauthor, *My Jesus Journal* and *Everyday Emmanuel*

"The most profound truths are often best communicated through great stories. *PROOF Pirates* weaves a tale that sails into uncharted water for children's books—a story that illustrates the goodness of God's grace over behavior management and performance-based praise. Timothy Paul Jones has long been an expert in family-equipping ministry, but what I love about him has always been his ability to combine deep theological insights with practical and fun ways to learn; this combination is clearer than ever in the family worship guides that accompany this story. A parent reading this well-illustrated book to their child will discover a treasure chest full of gospel truths for the scallywag in all of us, not just our kids."

JAY STROTHER, Campus and Teaching Pastor, The Church at Station Hill

"I read *PROOF Pirates* with my kids after dinner. I was going to read a little each day, but they made me finish it in one sitting. They were eager to find the treasure, and they weren't disappointed with what they discovered. For kids and parents alike, *PROOF* is a clear and compelling journey into the depths of God's grace!"

WILL WALKER, Pastor of Providence Church, Austin, TX; coauthor of *The Gospel-Centered Life*

"Stories are great conveyers of truth which is why Jesus so often told stories to his followers. His stories were often simple, repeatable, and powerful. Children of all ages won't be able to put this book down because the truths revealed are timeless!"

STEVE WRIGHT, Pastor of Discipleship and Church Planting, Family Church, West Palm Beach, FL

"I'm a big fan of making God's truth fun and memorable for families. Why not do so in a beautifully illustrated and easy to read resource? My seven-year-old son was on the edge of his seat on every page, listening to an adventure about God's incredible grace for you and me. His take: 'Really cool!' My take: 'Praise God!' Excellent resource for churches and families!"

CHRIS YOUNG, Pastor of Teaching and Families, Central Baptist Church, Warner Robins, GA; founder of www. childrensministrynetwork.com

PROOF PIRATES

✦ FAMILY DEVOTIONAL ✦

FINDING THE TREASURE OF GOD'S AMAZING GRACE

LINDSEY BLAIR, TIMOTHY PAUL JONES, AND JONAH SAGE

ILLUSTRATED BY TESSA JANES

New
Growth
Press

New Growth Press, Greensboro, NC 27404

PROOF Pirates was written to complement the book, *PROOF: Finding Freedom through the Intoxicating Joy of Irresistible Grace* by Daniel Montgomery and Timothy Paul Jones (Zondervan, 2014)

Cover and interior design by Faceout Studio

Library of Congress Cataloging-in-Publication Data

Blair, Lindsey, 1979-
  PROOF pirates : finding the treasure of God's amazing grace family devotional / Lindsey Blair, Timothy Paul Jones, Jonah Sage.
    pages cm
  ISBN 978-1-939946-65-2 (print) -- ISBN 978-1-939946-62-1 (ebook)
1. Families--Religious life. 2. Christian education of children. 3. Christian education--Home training.
4. Families--Prayers and devotions. 5. Grace (Theology)--Miscellanea. 6. Pirates--Miscellanea. I. Title.
  BV4526.3.B64 2015
  249--dc23
                              2015011858

Printed in China

22 21 20 19 18 17 16 15   1 2 3 4 5

INTRODUCTION

"For it is by grace you have been saved, through faith—and this is not from yourselves, it is the gift of God—not by works, so that no one can boast."

EPHESIANS 2:8–9

Chore charts, report cards, standardized tests, recitals, athletic banquets: the overwhelming message to kids is that what they do determines who they are. Kids grow up thinking, "I am what I am because of what I do. . .or because of what I've failed to do." But this message of performance is different from the Bible's message of redemption. In 1 Corinthians 15:10, Paul writes, "By the grace of God, I am what I am." In other words, what God says about me is more important than what others say.

The message of grace is that what we do or what we look like does not determine who we are as Christians. What God has determined for us through the work of his Son Jesus makes us who we are. We are loved even when our performance doesn't stack up. After all, Jesus came to save sinners—not those who get everything right.

PROOF Pirates family devotional is geared to the elementary-aged child. It has been designed to serve as a tool to help kids grasp and memorize five aspects of God's grace.

In the story, Jesse loves to pretend to be a scallywag, but finds that it gets him in a lot of trouble. He feels that everyone—even God—is disappointed with him. His parents want Jesse to get a clearer picture of God's love, which overcomes rebellion and circumstances. They want him to understand that the gospel is his greatest treasure.

This is what we want our kids to understand too. We want them to know that it is not their performance, but grace, that makes them right with God.

This book belongs to:

_____

Jesse, sword in hand, stepped into the living room. . .

With its big open space in the middle and the ocean blue rug, it was a tempting place to play pirate. He stopped and listened carefully; all was quiet. "Shiver me timbers, I have this part of the house to myself," he murmured with a mischievous grin. "I know Mom doesn't want me to play in here . . . but it's raining outside. Aargh . . . today I'm a scallywag."

He lunged onto the deck of the Spanish brig, sword outstretched, yelling, "Avast ye buccaneers . . ."

A grand sweep of his sword was followed by a crack and a crash. Jesse stared in horror at Mom's precious clock in pieces on the floor. He had disobeyed, and now the clock was broken! Jesse heard a gasp, and turned to see Mom and Dad standing in the archway behind him. They were not smiling.

Jesse apologized to his parents and asked for their forgiveness, but his disobedience still had consequences—an early bedtime. Jesse knew his parents had forgiven him. But he still felt awful.

As Jesse lay in bed, he opened his favorite pirate book. He thought, "I loved the idea of being a pirate, sword-fighting, and pretending to be a scallywag. It seemed like it would be fun. But now I'm suffering the consequences of BEING a scallywag. I disobeyed Mom and Dad—and now Mom's clock is broken. I feel really bad. Why am I always doing the wrong thing? Maybe there's no hope for me to be anything BUT a scallywag." Closing the book and turning off the light, Jesse closed his eyes, and prayed that tomorrow would be a better day.

The next morning, when Jesse came down for breakfast, Mom smiled and said, "Jesse, how would you like to go on a treasure hunt today?"

"Yes, yes, yes!" Jesse exclaimed jumping up and down in excitement.

Dad said, "Get ready by putting on your pirate costume."

Placing a gentle hand on Jesse's arm, his father continued, "Son, one more thing: Just remember that we are all sinners— parents too. Even though we sometimes choose to disobey, God still loves us and has given us a gift to save us and help us.

This hunt will help you learn more about that gift. It will give you proof of God's love and grace."

Jesse flew downstairs to the costume box in the family room. Mom and Dad were not far behind.

Once downstairs, Jesse opened the costume box, grabbed his pirate costume and quickly put it on. Bending down to pick up his bandanna, he noticed a folded sheet of paper rolled up inside it. Wondering what it could be, he removed the paper and carefully opened it.

It was a treasure map—a map of his house and yard! The title read "God's Grace Is . . ." Jesse examined the map and noticed scattered on it, five boxes. One box was labeled Clue 1, another box was labeled Clue 2, and so on for Clues 3, 4, and 5. The first box had a word already written in it: "Planned."

Mom, pointing to the title, read, "God's Grace Is. . . Do you see this blank space, Jesse? As you fill in the missing clues in the clue boxes, you can add the clue word to the title to find out more about God's grace." Then pointing to the "Clue 1" box she continued, "See Jesse, God's grace is *planned*. Before God created the heavens and earth, he had a plan. God mapped out salvation for us." After a pause, Mom continued, "Jesse, look at the map. Where will you find Clue 2?"

Jesse studied the map. "It looks like Clue 2 is somewhere in my room," he said.

"OK, let's go see," Dad said.

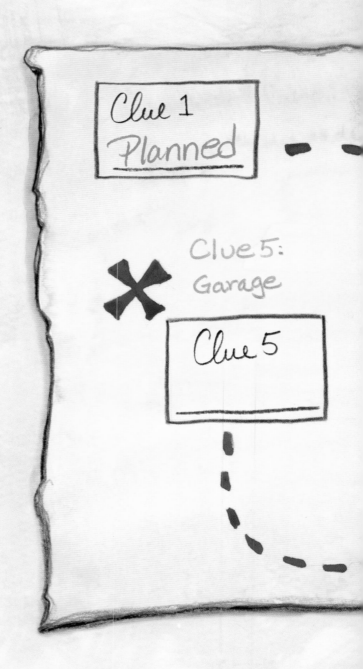

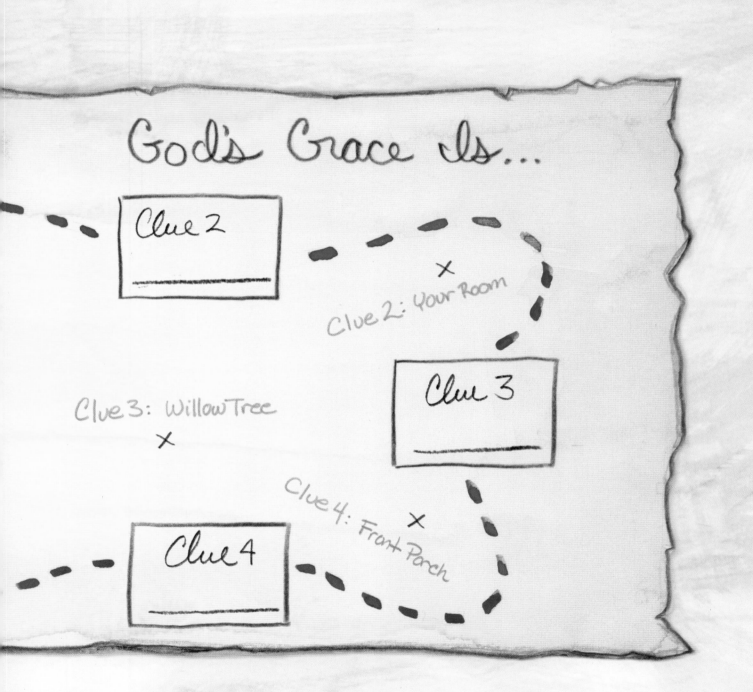

God's Grace Is...

Clue 2
_____

Clue 2: Your Room

Clue 3: Willow Tree

Clue 3
_____

Clue 4: Front Porch

Clue 4
_____

Once upstairs, Jesse entered his room, stopped and looked around. "Where's the clue?" he wondered aloud. "What is the clue?"

Nothing was changed since he had left his room for breakfast. The bed was still the same. The dresser, the same. Nothing different on the bookcase either. Then his eyes fell on the closet. "Hmm. . .I wonder. . ." he said moving to open the closet door.

As he swung the door open, he gasped, "What's this! What's my old skeleton costume doing hanging here!"

He glanced over his shoulder and noticed his parents standing in the bedroom doorway smiling. "Well, shiver me timbers," said Dad, "You found the next clue!"

Jesse laughed. Turning back to the skeleton, Jesse looked at it carefully and noticed, pinned to it, the words "Clue 2—Resurrecting." Jesse smiled.

"Here, Jesse, take this pencil and write the word 'Resurrecting' on the map in the box labeled clue 2," said Mom. "The Bible says that we are dead in our sin, but God makes us alive in Christ Jesus. When we were dead in sin, God made us alive!"

As Jesse wrote, he thought about God bringing a dead person back to life! He thought about all his foolish choices. He realized that it did not matter how hard he tried, he could not obey his parents without God's help. He wanted to know more about how God could make him alive.

"Where's the next clue?" Dad asked.

Looking at the map, Jesse said, "It looks like it's outside in the yard under the willow tree. Let's go!"

Jesse stood in the yard near the willow tree. He looked at the map as he walked slowly around the tree. "The clue has to be here somewhere," he said. The map clearly showed the third clue in the backyard next to a tree, but Jesse didn't see it!

Dad said, "Don't forget that pirates sometimes bury treasure."

Walking slowly around the tree, looking carefully at the ground, Jesse suddenly saw some grass cut away in the shape of a small X. That was it! "Mom, Dad, I think I need a shovel!" Jesse exclaimed.

"Like this one?" Dad said as he handed Jesse a small shovel that had been lying behind a nearby shrub.

Jesse took the shovel and began to dig on the spot marked with the X. Very soon the shovel made a clanking sound as it struck something solid just below the surface.

"Mom, Dad, something's here!" Removing just a few more shovelfuls of dirt revealed a small box, which Jesse lifted out and showed to his parents. Setting it on the ground, Jesse moved the latch and the top opened easily. "Look, a. . .a cross! It has some writing on it." Looking closely at the small cross, Jesse read, "Clue 3—Out. . . Outrage. . ." Holding up the cross Jesse asked, "Mom, Dad, what's this word?"

"Jesse, the word is outrageous," Dad said. "God loved you and me before we were even born. There's nothing we can do on

our own to be saved. God doesn't love us because we do good things or because we are born into a good family. God loved us first. He saves us because of everything that HE has done and nothing that WE have done. That's hard for us to imagine. God's grace is outrageous!"

Jesse wrote the word "outrageous" on the map in the box labeled clue 3. Then he said, "I think I get it. The cross marks the spot! Jesus is our treasure, our free gift. So far I've learned that God's grace is *Planned* and *Resurrecting* and *Outrageous*."

Continuing to look at the map, Jesse said, "It looks like the next clue is on the front porch. Let's go see!"

Jesse climbed the porch steps and looked around wondering what the next clue could be. There weren't many hiding places on the porch. Jesse checked the mailbox, but it was empty. Then he peered down the side of the large planter, but, again, nothing. He walked the length of the porch and noticed a white cloth draped over the swing. He picked up the white cloth and sat down on the swing, thinking about what the white cloth might represent. Then, he remembered from battle stories that you wave a white flag when you want to surrender. Suddenly, Mom and Dad shouted, "Jesse, prepare for a water fight!"

Mom and Dad burst out laughing and started shooting Jesse with water pistols. Jesse laughed and quickly picked up the white cloth to protect himself from being sprayed. "I surrender!" he shouted. "I'm waving my white flag! I surrender!"

"That's exactly right!" said Dad.

Spreading out the flag to get a better look, Jesse read, "clue 4—Overcoming." He took out his map and pencil and began to write in the box labeled clue 4.

While Jesse wrote, Dad explained, "God's grace is *Overcoming* because it can't be resisted. God changes our pirate flag of rebellion into a white flag of surrender. The more we know about the goodness and greatness of salvation in Jesus, the more irresistible he becomes.

Though we are disobedient sinners who run away from God, he has come near to us. When our eyes are opened and we begin to understand how amazing God's grace is, we do not want to rebel any longer."

Finished writing, Jesse examined the map. "There's only one more empty box. And it looks like it's in the garage!" Map in hand, he jumped off the porch and took off across the yard.

In front of the garage, Jesse stopped short, mouth open in amazement. "Mom! Dad!" he shouted. "The boat! It look's like a pirate ship!! There's a sail, a flag with skull and crossbones, and look, even my stuffed parrot!" In a flash he had climbed on board, exclaiming, "Ahoy, matey!"

Once on board, he looked around trying to figure out what the next clue was. Before long he noticed a sign attached to the boat anchor. Detaching the sign he waved it at his parents.

"Mom! Dad! Look what was attached to the anchor. It says, 'Forever.' This is the last clue, isn't it!" He sat down, took out his map, and carefully printed "Forever" in the last empty box.

Why the anchor? He wondered to himself. He knew that an anchor keeps a boat safe from drifting away. Jesse had a hunch the anchor was about how God would keep him safe and secure as well.

Mom said, "You know, Jesse, once you become a child of God, you will always be his. God gives his people the Holy Spirit. The Holy Spirit is like our anchor. He keeps us so that we never drift away from his love."

Dad said, "Jesse, you can play on the boat until lunchtime. Have fun!" And a lot of fun he had too, playing on his very own pirate ship.

When Jesse came in for lunch, Dad said, "Jesse, let's take one more look at that map."

Jesse unfolded it and placed it on the table. Handing him a pencil, Mom said, "Jesse there's one more thing to do. On the bottom of the map, print the first letter of each of the clues. Write them in order from one to five.

Jesse did just that. He quickly noticed that the first letters of the clues—*Planned, Resurrecting, Outrageous, Overcoming,* and *Forever*—written in order spelled out the word PROOF.

Jesse hugged his parents and thanked them for sharing PROOF of God's amazing grace. He thought back to the night before, when he broke his mother's special clock,

and how horrible he felt. He knew that he had disobeyed his parents and sinned against them. He knew that he would sin again, but now he also knew that God loved him even when he sinned. He realized that God's love was changing him. He didn't want to run away from obeying God and his parents anymore. He wanted to follow God and run into his arms of love.

FAMILY DEVOTIONAL I: WAKE UP TO GRACE!

But God demonstrates his own love for us in this: While we were still sinners, Christ died for us.

ROMANS 5:8

God's love is amazing. He loved us when we were sinners, when we were his enemies. God didn't wait for us to clean ourselves up. He showed his love by sending Jesus to die for us.

Work it out: **Find a buried treasure.**

Take something your children would be excited about (a toy, piece of candy, etc.) and bury it somewhere in your yard. (If it's a piece of food, make sure to put in a secure container.) Create a simple treasure map for your children. If you're feeling especially creative, put some costumes on and then go hunt for the treasure. When you find the treasure, it will be covered with dirt. Take time to wash the treasure (or its container). After it is washed, enjoy it.

Read it: Read Luke 15:1–10.

Talk about it:

Do you ever feel like a failure?

What does the Bible tell us we were like when God chose to love us?

Do we have to make ourselves clean before God will love us?

How does God show that he loves us?

Hide it in your heart: Memorize Romans 5:8 (at the top of the page); memorize the following question/answer.

Question: What is God's grace?

Answer: God's grace is his love freely given to us in Jesus.

Pray: Father, thank you for loving us when we were still sinners. Thank you for sending Jesus to find us when we were lost. Amen.

FAMILY DEVOTIONAL 2: PLANNED GRACE

For he chose us in him before the creation of the world. . .In love, he predestined us.

EPHESIANS 1:4-5a

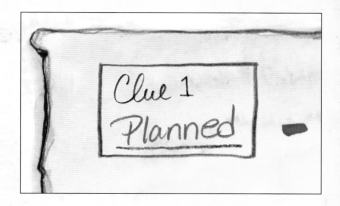

Before God made the heavens and the earth, he had a plan. God mapped out salvation for the people he loves. That's what the word <u>predestined</u> means. God picked out whom he would save, and he decided just how he would save them. God's plan was fully accomplished when Jesus died on the cross.

Work it out: **Build a pirate ship!**

Start with a large appliance box, which can be found at a hardware or appliance store. Remove one long side from the box and set it on the ground. Work with your kids to paint or draw a ship on the side of the box with markers. Finally, cut a triangle out of an old sheet or t-shirt, and tape it to a broom handle or stick. Attach that to the box. When your ship is complete, go on board your homemade vessel for your adventure at sea. Feel free to spray each other with water bottles, or use buckets to "bail out" the ship. (If possible, save the ship to use in a later lesson.)

Read it: Read Acts 27:13–44.

Talk about it:

Why wasn't Paul worried for his safety?

What does it take to make a plan? Hint: think about how you plan to go grocery shopping.

Who is the best planner?

How does it make you feel that God loves you and has a plan for you?

Hide it in your heart: Memorize Ephesians 1:4–5a
(at the top of the page); memorize the following definition and question/answer.

Planned Grace: God mapped out salvation for his people.

Question: When did God choose to love and save his people?

Answer: God planned to love and save his people before the creation of the world.

Pray: Father, thank you for loving us and making a plan to save your people before the world began. Amen.

FAMILY DEVOTIONAL 3: RESURRECTING GRACE

But because of his great love for us, God, who is rich in mercy, made us alive with Christ even when we were dead in transgressions—it is by grace you have been saved.

EPHESIANS 2:4–5

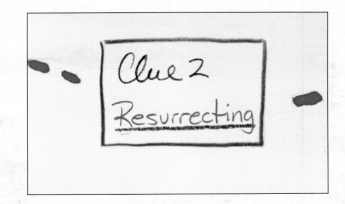

The Bible says that we cannot follow God without God's help. We are like dead skeletons. Dead skeletons have no muscles, no brain, and no heart. They have no power to move on their own. But God can make those dead skeletons live again. God can make dead men and women and boys and girls walk in obedience to him. The Bible says that God makes us alive in Christ Jesus. He gives us power to make wise choices, power to obey him, power to live.

Work it out: Dead and alive.

Have your kids pretend to be dead—tell them to be perfectly silent and still. Can a dead person move? Talk? Get up and walk? Say, "We were dead in our sins." Then, shout out, "But God made us alive!" Everyone jump up and dance around because you're alive! Say, "We're not skeletons! God has made us alive!" *Practice it again and again as you say the memory verse.*

Read it: Read Ezekiel 37:1–14.

Talk about it:
• What did Jesse find in his closet?

• Can a dead skeleton dance around without muscles and a brain to help it?

• Can we obey God's voice without his help?

• What happened when Ezekiel preached to the bones?

Hide it in your heart: Memorize Ephesians 2:4–5 (at the top of the page); memorize the following definition and question/answer.

Resurrecting Grace: When we were dead, God made us alive!

Question: Can you come to God in your own power?

Answer: No, we are dead in sin, and we need the Holy Spirit to make us alive.

Pray: Holy Spirit, we are dead without you. We need you to come and make us alive. Amen.

FAMILY DEVOTIONAL 4: OUTRAGEOUS GRACE

In him we have redemption through his blood, the forgiveness of sins, in accordance with the riches of God's grace that he lavished on us.

EPHESIANS 1:7–8a

To redeem something means to buy it back—to pay a price so you can have it back. God paid the price for our sins by sending his Son, Jesus Christ, to die on the cross. There is nothing we can do to earn or deserve God's grace. God gives us Jesus as a free gift! God doesn't love us because we do good things or because we were born into a good family. God loved us first—before we did anything good or bad. God loves us because Jesus paid the price for us. He redeemed us.

Work it out: **Build a treasure chest.**

Collect a small box —a shoebox works well—for each child. Gather craft supplies, e.g., crayons, markers, paint, stickers, construction paper, etc. Have your children decorate the treasure chest as they wish.

Read it: Read Deuteronomy 10:14–15.

Talk about it:

- Why did you choose to decorate the treasure chest the way that you did? Hint: Be specific. For example, why did you choose the pink stickers?

- How much money would you pay for that treasure chest?

- Did you know that God made you his special treasure?

- How much did God pay for us to be his treasure?

Hide it in your heart: Memorize Ephesians 1:7–8a (at the top of the page); memorize the following definition and question/answer.

Outrageous Grace: God gives us Jesus as a free gift!

Question: What is an enemy of God's grace?

Answer: An enemy of God's grace is the lie that we're good enough or that we can work hard enough to earn God's love.

Pray: Lord Jesus, thank you for paying the full price for our sins. Amen.

FAMILY DEVOTIONAL 5: OVERCOMING GRACE

"My sheep listen to my voice; I know them, and they follow me."

JOHN 10:27

God does for us what we can't do for ourselves. God gives us his Spirit to overcome our sin even when we can't change our minds on our own.

Work it out: **A treasure hunt**.

Buy some chocolate gold coins and hide them inside or out. Hide at least one coin in an obvious place where *you* can reach it but your children cannot. Let them hunt for a while and then stop them and ask why they don't grab that one coin. When they realize they are unable to reach it on their own, reach up and grab it for them. Tell them that God does for us what we can't do for ourselves. Choosing not to sin is out of our reach just like that high gold coin was. Just like I reached the coin for you, God is gracious and gives us his Spirit to overcome our sin even when we can't change our minds on our own. In today's Bible story Saul wasn't looking for Jesus. He was looking to hurt Jesus's people, but Jesus found him.

Read it: Read Acts 9:1–22.

Talk about it:

• How did it feel to need help to reach the coin that was up high?

• Have you ever been unable to do something you know you should do? For example, have you ever been unable to forgive someone for something even though you know God wants you to?

• Has knowing God's overcoming love ever helped you to love someone else? Parent: Be prepared to share an example from your own life.

Hide it in your heart: Memorize John 10:27 (at the top of the page); memorize the following definition and question/answer.

Overcoming Grace: God changes our rebellion into surrender.

Question: Who will come to God?

Answer: We can't reach God, but he reaches us.

Pray: Father, change my heart when I want to do wrong. Give me an overcoming love for you. Amen.

FAMILY DEVOTIONAL 6: FOREVER GRACE

When you believed, you were marked in him with a seal, the promised Holy Spirit, who is a deposit guaranteeing our inheritance.

EPHESIANS 1:13b–14a

Today's Bible passage calls the Holy Spirit a seal—a special mark. Because of the Holy Spirit, God's people are marked as his children forever. God protects his children so they can never be lost. God always finishes the work he begins in us. Even though life is sometimes like sailing on a stormy sea, God is with us, and he protects us. He brings us back to himself like a boat that has been guided safely to shore.

Work it out: Lost on a desert island.

Set aside an area inside or out to serve as the "desert island." If you still have the pirate ship from the "Planned Grace" devotional, have the kids hop in. If not, just have them pretend to sail around. Stock the desert island with some of a pirate's favorite snacks. Fish sticks or goldfish crackers work great! Once your pirates have had enough sailing, pretend that they are shipwrecked on the island. Let them enjoy their snacks. While they eat ask them what they would do if they *really* were shipwrecked on a deserted island. Ask them what they would do if they ran out of food and had no way to call for help. Tell them that God never deserts us—God's love holds onto them and keeps them forever.

Read it: Read John 10:27–30.

Talk about it:

How long is forever? What lasts forever?

How do you know that God loves you?

Hide it in your heart: Memorize Ephesians 1:13b–14a (at the top of the page); memorize the following definition and question/answer.

Forever Grace: God's people never drift away from his love.

Question: How do I know that I belong to God?

Answer: The Holy Spirit marks us as God's children forever.

Pray: God, thank you for finishing the work you began in me. Your love never fails. Amen.

FAMILY DEVOTIONAL 7: GRACE FOR LIFE

For it is by grace you have been saved, through faith—and this is not from yourselves, it is the gift of God—not by works, so that no one can boast.

EPHESIANS 2:8-9

Review the five key aspects of God's grace with your kids:

- **Planned Grace:** God mapped out salvation for his people.

- **Resurrecting Grace:** When we were dead, God made us alive.

- **Outrageous Grace:** God gives us Jesus as a free gift!

- **Overcoming Grace:** God changes our rebellion into surrender.

- **Forever Grace:** God's people never drift away from his love.

Work it out: Masterpiece of grace.
In Ephesians 2:10 we read that those who believe in Jesus are God's handiwork—his masterpiece! He made us to do the good works that he already had prepared for us to do. Grab some poster board, markers, stickers, and paints. Then, write the word PROOF down the left side of the poster. Work with your children to create a poster that explains all five aspects of God's grace. Display it as a reminder that we are God's handiwork—his masterpiece.

Read it: Read Ephesians 2:1–10.

Talk about it:
What do you think is the most valuable masterpiece in the entire world?

How does it make you feel to know that you are God's masterpiece—saved by his amazing grace?

Hide it in your heart: Memorize Ephesians 2:8–9 (at the top of the page).

Pray: God, help me to believe that what you say about me is more true and important than what anyone else says. Thank you for your amazing grace! Amen.